THE WORLD
ACCORDING TO
BLOFELD'S
CAT

UNOFFICIAL

**MUSINGS
FROM THE
VOLCANO
LAIR**

'There's more than a little of Ian Fleming himself in Blofeld's Cat as he at last emerges from his volcano lair to put the world to rights. The perfect gift for the Bond villain in your family.'
Matthew Parker, author of *Goldeneye: Where Bond was Born – Ian Fleming's Jamaica*

'I'm not sure if there's a cat flap big enough for this feline's ego.'
Mark O'Connell, author of *Catching Bullets: Memoirs of a Bond Fan*

'My cat makes Pol Pot and Stalin look like a pair of social reformers.'
Number 1

'My book is outrageously good.'
Blofeld's Cat

THE WORLD ACCORDING TO BLOFELD'S CAT

UNOFFICIAL

MUSINGS FROM THE VOLCANO LAIR

Words by Blofeld's Cat
with Mark Beynon, Alistair Beynon and Chris Paull

Illustrations and cover artwork by Blofeld's Cat
with Adrian Teal

tumbleweed

To Number 1, with love

First published 2015
by Tumbleweed, an imprint of The History Press
The Mill, Brimscombe Port,
Stroud, Gloucestershire, GL5 2QG
www.thehistorypress.co.uk

British Library Cataloguing in Publication Data.
A catalogue record for this book is available from the British Library.

ISBN 978 0 7509 5961 2

Design by Katie Beard
Printed and bound in Great Britain by TJ International Ltd

BLOFELD'S CAT is not a charming street cat who has won the hearts of a nation; nor is he a cute, cuddly house cat with a bell attached to his collar, who happily chases a ball of string around a room. He is, however, a narcissistic, indignant, scheming, acerbic, brilliant, sociopath of a cat, whose lavish tastes and desire for destruction are unprecedented. He lives in a hollowed-out volcano lair in an unspecified location. This is his first book.

Disclaimer
The views and opinions expressed herein are those of the author and do not necessarily reflect those of the publisher. Especially the bit on contemporary music. Likewise, the names included herein have been changed to protect the identities of the real idiots.

ACKNOWLEDGEMENTS

I should begin by saying that it was never my intention to have this collection of cogitations published. In actual fact, the idea initially struck me as being vulgar in the extreme – that was until a feckless publisher offered me a vast sum of money, at which point I hastily changed my mind. Accordingly, I ought to thank my esteemed colleague Number 10, who encouraged me to seek help apropos my rage, thus inspiring this twee little anthology of hatred you have in your hands. If it weren't for his suggestion I would still be inserting sticks of dynamite into helpless mice and using them as crude grenades. My agent, the beautiful and incomparable Penny Dreadful, has been a constant source of encouragement. My aforementioned publishers, who, despite their best efforts, have somehow managed to produce a book that isn't a complete disaster. And finally, to Number 1, who not only took me in as a stray and let me kill people, but who also resisted the urge to call me Snuffles, Mr Whiskers or something equally crass. It's been quite a journey!

FOREWORD

As a self-confessed despotic megalomaniac hell-bent on world domination, I never pictured myself owning a pet, least of all a fluffy white cat. And even if I did, the old axiom of a pet taking on its owner's personality would surely never apply to me. How could it? After all, domesticated pets are docile, loving and peaceful creatures. Well, it

soon transpired that I was grossly mistaken. When I acquired the cat as a stray to keep down the rats at our old Parisian HQ, early on it became apparent that he wasn't just killing the vermin, he was also torturing them. He would turn his nose up at the food we gave him, unless it was lovingly prepared by the finest chefs, and would routinely eschew any liquid refreshment that wasn't vintage claret. Other pets residing at HQ would go out of their way to avoid him – we even once found him choking Number 4's mastiff, Napoleon, with a telephone cord. So when Number 9 politely enquired as to whether we could return the cat to the street (where he couldn't do any further harm), I had the snivelling little weasel electrocuted and the cat promoted from rat-catching duties. Since then he has proved to be an invaluable ally, despite the escalating veterinary bills, and this compendium of his miserable musings acts as a permanent reminder to me why he's not just my pet cat, but also my best friend.

Number 1
A volcano lair, location unspecified
January 2015

INTRODUCTION

Over the past few years it has become increasingly apparent to me that the older I get, the angrier and more disdainful towards humanity I come to be. Naturally, I don't blame myself for this slide into perpetual misanthropy, not in the slightest. I often find myself wondering how and why society has become so indolent and ineffectual. Is it the ongoing sullying of the gene pool? Or has technology and innovation played a key role in shaping the slow-witted society of tomorrow?

My psychiatrist suggested that the best way to treat this malaise was to write down my thoughts on what exasperates me most. What transpired was a wonderfully cathartic experience – an experience that I would wholeheartedly recommend to anyone who, like me, abhors mankind and has a genuine sense of foreboding for what the future may bring.

I have led a wonderfully exciting life; I've travelled extensively and experienced things that most other cats can only dream of. Perhaps this is the reason why I now feel a little lost, like a stopped clock or an empty vase. Either way, I want to enjoy the twilight of my existence and look back with fondness on my many cherished memories, not be angered by the amount of spam in my inbox or the increasing volume of automated PPI calls to my mobile phone.

Blofeld's Cat
January 2015

REALITY TELEVISION

This modern propensity that television producers have for abandoning a collection of 'celebrities', who we all thought were long dead, into increasingly peculiar scenarios is both demeaning (for the 'celebrity') and highly irritating (for the viewer). I have written numerous missives to the slipshod production companies outlining my thoughts on how they can improve their respective shows. This is the email response I received from the bed-wetters at Hoojoo Productions following my latest communiqué.

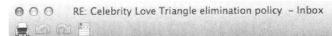

Message

RE: Celebrity Love Triangle elimination policy

Chris Sharp <csharp@hoojooproductions.com>

Sent: Tue 24/02/15 10:05

To: Blofeld's Cat

Dear Mr Cat,

Thank you for your recent email regarding your thoughts on our show *Celebrity Love Triangle*. Whilst we actively encourage all viewers to get in touch with reasonable and constructive suggestions on how we can best develop our programming, following legal advice we have forwarded your barbaric comments to the police. Your suggestion that we should improve our 'outstayed and tedious' elimination policy by giving viewers the chance to vote for the contestants to be 'showered in petrol and conflagrated instead' was both malicious and downright disturbing. Rest assured the authorities will be pursuing this matter further.

Yours sincerely,

Chris Sharp
Producer, Hoojoo Productions

BINGE DRINKING

Ah, alcohol. The elixir of life. I love a glass of wine with every meal, including breakfast, and I can't remember the last time I had a nap without a preceding brandy. In fact, my milk bowl has been rather bereft of milk of late …

I'm often known to imbibe a little too much, perhaps more often than I'd care to admit. It's a consequence of my enthusiasm for the finer things in life. What I can't abide, though, is drinking for drinking's sake – the hobby *du jour* of these foul-mouthed yobs who regularly indulge in vast quantities of inexpensive, mass-produced, artificial poison, only to then behave even more moronically. I recall one incident, after a particularly decadent late-night carousal, when I had the misfortune of being greeted by just such a group of knuckle-dragging Neanderthals, who thought it would be amusing to kick me around like a football. They were wrong, as they discovered when I had them bound to a railway line. Since then I've taken great care to avoid groups of inebriated imbeciles, for their sake and mine.

JUNK MAIL

After recently returning home from a splendid vacation in the Bahamas, I could barely fit through my cat flap for the mountain of junk mail that had piled up on the doormat in my absence. With the exception of a couple of utility bills that had reached 'final warning' status, the rest consisted of cheaply produced direct marketing leaflets for a variety of deplorable products and services. Apart from one. I must admit that curiosity nearly killed me as I excitedly thumbed my way through the wonderfully varied à la carte menu for 'King Goobler's Kebab Emporium'. His bucket of spicy chicken wings looked particularly delightful, and a real bargain, too. However, upon speaking with the 'emporium' in question, I was saddened to discover that King Goobler wasn't a real monarch, but was, in fact, a Turkish former wrestler called Hassan. As I struggled to contain my disappointment, I informed Mr Goobler that, whilst I applauded his business acumen, if I received another menu from his execrable establishment I would be forced to commit high treason by having the 'king' deep fried in his own 'special batter'.

THE BRITISH SECRET SERVICE

The British Secret Service: as malingering as they are ugly, and populated by hundreds of sickly-looking, bespectacled individuals, all of whom display the social graces of an ungainly pigeon.

Having had many run-ins with them over the years, I believe I am well versed in how they approach their work. To give them their due, there was one chap in particular (whom for legal reasons I cannot name) who had an irritating knack of thwarting some of our finest schemes. The last I heard, our bête noire was living on his own in a studio apartment in Leighton Buzzard, having spent a small fortune on child maintenance and penicillin.

GYMS

Nothing will turn me into a miserable curmudgeon quite as quickly as a visit to the gym. Although I really ought to lose some blubber from my midriff, I'd rather die a bloated mess than spend another minute in a clammy room full of preening tossers, whose abundance of muscle fails to make up for their dramatic shortfall of brain cells and personality. If watching these vest-clad aberrations perform their grotesque routines wasn't bad enough, having to withstand their pre- and post-gym 'banter' in the changing room whilst they thrust their testicles in each other's faces is beyond the pale. If I had a desire to witness such behaviour I would visit a homoerotic cabaret.

LOCAL NEWS

Local newspapers afford me endless entertainment, no matter which country I find myself residing in. I had some spare time recently so I used it to pen the somewhat disingenuous letter below to the fine people of the *Danbridge Mercury*, a regional rag in southern England. The letter is yet to be published.

SIR

May I take the opportunity to congratulate you and your colleagues on your continued cutting-edge journalism that assists the authorities in ridding the streets of Danbridge of the villainous skulduggery that blights this otherwise beguiling corner of old England? If there was a Pulitzer Prize handed out to local journalists, then surely Christopher Croucher's piece in last week's *Mercury* under the headline 'BIRTHDAY CARD THIEF SOUGHT' would've earned him the accolade. Mr Croucher bravely chose not to seek anonymity in the article in which he cautioned his readers, in his usual florid prose, to be vigilant should they spot an 'olive-skinned man with a handlebar moustache rifling through their unopened birthday cards'. Quite why this story wasn't picked up by the national press is a mystery, as I'm sure it has left those denizens of Danbridge whose birthdays will soon be upon them quaking with fear. Of course, it was Mr Croucher who earlier in the year warned his readers of the perils of the 'DANBRIDGE SPROUT WARS' and (who could possibly forget?!) vile 'CLIVE, THE PEEPING TOM', so the quality of his latest exposé shouldn't come as a surprise to those who ardently follow his journalistic endeavours. Keep up the good work, Mr Croucher. Your village depends on you.

Yours (very) sincerely,

Mr Blofeld's Cat, Esq.

CHRISTMAS

Christmas: the hateful festive season in which parents notify their progenies that whilst they sleep a bearded old stranger will be entering their bedrooms unaccompanied. Indeed, there is much to detest about Yuletide, which is heralded by a) your cretinous neighbour festooning his bungalow in a myriad of nuclear-powered lights that are visible from space; b) the arrival of the obligatory round-robin letter from a self-righteous family you've long despised, whose insistence on putting their annual highlights on paper is absolutely galling (honestly, I couldn't care less if Sebastian overcame his nut allergy or if Drusilla triumphed in the school egg-and-spoon race); and c) an influx of ludicrous perfume adverts that are completely unintelligible. And if that's not traumatic enough, there's always the maelstrom of monotonous music that makes you want to crush the larynx of mankind, as well as the pointless exchanging of gift-wrapped tat with fools you'd gladly harpoon to their own Christmas trees.

But it's the godawful food I find most offensive of all. No one should have turkey forced upon them, not even the feral cats that exist purely on a diet of

polluted air and stagnant water. In all seriousness, I would sooner consume the grit that is unfortunate enough to line my litter tray. What's wrong with a festive Côte de Boeuf washed down with a robust Château Latour '82 for pity's sake? I'm sure the Baby Jesus would have approved.

And just when you think it's all over for another year, you wake up to Boxing Day – the day when the peasant underclass queue outside some wretched department store en masse in the hope of getting 20 per cent off matching pyjamas. Utter lunacy.

I'm always glad to see January – a cold, bleak, unforgiving time of year that really slaps the common man in the face, especially when they open their credit card statements from the previous month. No more merriment for you, Mr Cratchitt from Camden. Social Services will be around shortly to remove Tiny Tim from your revolting family. And you can tell those three ghosts to sod off. Bah, humbug!

TEXT TALK

The laziness of the younger generation is displayed most disturbingly by their attitude towards communication (both verbal and written). I have no quarrel with mobile technology: in fact, I have learnt to embrace the wondrous advancements in recent years. However, I am continually alarmed by how the English language is being bastardised by hordes of spotty urchins, who are clearly more concerned with engaging in online warfare with children from Singapore (whose grasp of English is far superior to that of their English-speaking counterparts) than doing their homework. Some call it evolution; I call it bone idleness. Either way, 'text talk' (or 'txt tlk' for the brain dead) infuriates me more than being wormed. The beautiful English language of Shakespeare, Byron and Keats has been usurped by a series of crude misspellings and acronyms. OMG and WTF, I hear you say. Well, TBH, I am totes fed up. U shd b 2. FML.

WORLD PEACE

LOL.

CAT LITERATURE

It has recently come to my attention that there has been a sharp upturn in the number of published books in the sub-genre of 'Cat Humour'. Now, having suffered some of these publications, I habitually find myself marvelling at what sort of simpleton would willingly hand over £7.99 of their hard-earned money on an insipid and derivative collection of feline anecdotes? At least I am safe in the knowledge that my musings will be safely locked away. I could think of nothing worse than my words forming some tasteless compendium that is flaunted to the masses by a money-grabbing publisher, dining out on my good name to fund their wanton drinking habit. What a ghastly thought.*

*Written before I signed a contract with my publisher. Which is a bit awkward.

MURDER

OFTEN NECESSARY, FREQUENTLY ENJOYABLE, ALWAYS MESSY. ESPECIALLY WHEN MY DANDER IS UP.

ONLINE DATING

Certainly a step up from the lottery that is the lonely hearts column, I think it's rather charming that society's ogres now have a forum from which they can meet and elope, having been previously bound for a life of preordained celibacy. I say three cheers for the monsters in love (providing they don't procreate and risk further muddying the shallow waters of the gene pool, of course).

PACKAGE HOLIDAYS

The good old package holiday – where budget airlines transport the dregs of British society to an assortment of cheap and tawdry resorts around Europe each summer – offers the promise of fishbowl cocktails, foam parties and fornication with other chlamydia-riddled ne'er-do-wells. What their European cousins must make of these reprobates is anyone's guess, but I very much doubt they'd be invited back to stay with the Papazoglakis family for moussaka and ouzo at Christmas.

It's always a source of abject misery when one casts an eye around the departure lounges at British airports during the high season and spots the herds of oversexed twenty-somethings guffawing at each other's none-too-subtle 'tour t-shirts', upon the back of which such wonderfully crafted nicknames such as

'Turkey Tits' and 'Hoover Nostrils' are emblazoned. I am eternally hopeful that old 'Hoover Nostrils' is violated by airport security at Heraklion. That'll make him cry into his fishbowl.

BONFIRE NIGHT

Only in England would communities of ruddy-faced country folk converge on the village green to celebrate the burning effigy of a man who had the gumption to attempt to blow corrupt politicians and an incompetent monarch to smithereens. This ritual is prefaced by gaggles of malnourished children, resembling something from a Dickensian poorhouse, dragging this sorry-looking scarecrow around their village and begging for money. Clearly a 'penny for the Guy' has yielded to inflation, as anything less than a £1 donation is now looked upon with scorn.

And then the blasted fireworks arrive, accompanied by the groans of 'oooh' and 'aaah' from the throngs of slack-jawed farmhands, who look on in childlike wonderment as these rather pathetic bangers (fourth only to flowers, personalised number plates and greeting cards as the world's biggest waste of money) disappear in a cloud of coloured vapour. If I was impertinent enough to suggest an improvement to the festivities, I'd use actual explosives and blow a crater in the village green. It's what Guy Fawkes would've wanted.

CATTERIES

I often hear people use the word 'cattery' as if they're describing some sort of luxury hotel or guesthouse for my fellow brethren. How wildly incorrect they are! Whilst on first impression these feline prisons may seem rather pleasant, I can safely say that after spending a night trapped behind the cold, iron bars of solitude, enduring a diet of kippers and sour milk, and having to tolerate the wondrous experience of sleeping next to your own litter tray, it is not something I would happily repeat. This point is reinforced when you're 'housed' next to a tabby with severe flatulence or if you're forced to share a cell with one of the 'sisters'. Many cats break down on their first night – much to the delight of the more hard-nosed alley cats who have money riding on who will crack first. A pastime that helps to, well, pass the time.

RECRUITMENT AGENCIES

It has become progressively difficult to find the right people for our organisation, not least because of our laughably high staff turnover rate. Also, ideals have seemingly changed and treachery appears to be thin on the ground, resulting in us turning to specialist recruitment agencies to supply us with appropriately deviant candidates. Henchman Selection claim to be the best in the business at sourcing 'the perfect knuckleheads for you', although I beg to differ having just received this frankly absurd application.

HENCHMAN SELECTION INC.

Full name: David Andrew Syms
Nationality: British
Email: █████████████
Contact number: ███████████
Sex: Male
Date of birth: 13/06/89
Position applied for: Trainee Henchman
Education: Brenda's Dance Academy

Appropriate attributes for the position applied for: As a former professional dancer, I'm very lithe and have cat-like reflexes

Areas in which you can improve: I'm not particularly confrontational and will require combat and weapons training

Are you physically formidable?: LOL! No

Interests: Wildlife, reading, walking, human rights activism, environmentalism, musical theatre

Are you a member of any organisations or societies?: Amnesty International and Greenpeace

Do you hold a valid driving licence?: I don't drive as I'm opposed to carbon emissions

Previous employment: I toured as a dancer on numerous musical theatre productions before becoming a nursery school teacher

Availability: Currently unemployed

Desired hours: Afternoon

Preferred method of contact: Hugs and kisses!

SOCIAL MEDIA

If I'm honest, I'm about as familiar with the workings of social media as a white supremacist is with the inner machinations of the Bexley African-Caribbean Community Association. Nevertheless, I am at least trying to understand the modern-day proclivity to precede every witticism with a hashtag and fathom out why drunken delinquents delight in uploading videos of them regurgitating their supper to the amusement of their peers, all in the vain hope of becoming an overnight internet sensation. However, I have completely given up trying to comprehend those who insist on sharing endless pictures of their

Blofeld's Cat @realblofeldscat ·
Exciting plans at #SPECTRE HQ! We're having the old operations room turned into a bar for senior staff. I'm calling it The Disgruntled Cat.

↩   ⟳ 2   ★ 2   •••

Blofeld's Cat @realblofeldscat ·
Which numbskull brought a dog into work today? You have five minutes to remove it from HQ before I have it turned into a chair.

↩   ⟳ 2   ★   •••

corpulent babies, as well as the windbags who bore their friends/followers to death with a stream of self-indulgent, attention-seeking twaddle regarding their weight loss or, worse still, their inability to find love. (It's because you're an intolerable, fat wench, my dear.)

What I do find encouraging about social media is just how easy it is to build your own PR machine without having to spend a small fortune on agency fees. To that end, I have taken it upon myself to open my own Twitter handle – @realblofeldscat. Disappointingly, however, @mugabesdog and @kimjongunsrabbit are my only followers thus far.

CHILDREN

Odious little turds, the lot of them. There is quite literally nothing that will send me into a state of sheer panic more than being cornered by hordes of dribbling infants. No animal, not even a stray dog, deserves to be screamed at, beaten with a plastic spade, or have their fur ripped out in large clumps. It's an utterly degrading and miserable experience. Indeed, I've made moves to cancel our calamitous 'bring your kids to work day' at HQ before I feed someone's hideous child to the shark.

With that in mind, I'm currently in the advanced stages of devising my patented 'Shock Coat', an easy-to-wear device that will render any youth who touches me incapacitated for a full five minutes. I'm still awaiting feedback from Mothercare.

GHOSTS

It's very seldom I get the chance to commandeer the remote control at home, especially when Number 1 is watching a dismal programme called *The Spectre Detectors* in which a group of rumbustious charlatans — complete with a cerebrally challenged psychic medium called Ron — visit a series of allegedly haunted locations across the world and film themselves running aimlessly around in the dark. Such was his obsession with this loose stool of a show that he hired the aforesaid 'detectors' to perform a private ghost hunt at HQ (sans broadcast cameras!). When they predictably failed to find any evidence of ethereal activity, despite me walking around with a bed sheet over my head, Number 1 was left entirely deflated by the whole debacle. Somewhat ironically, the 'detectors' themselves are now said to haunt the bowels of HQ.

THE TOP 11 WORST PLACES I'VE EVER HAD THE MISFORTUNE TO VISIT

11. ISLE OF MAN

I flirted with the idea of moving our organisation to this peculiar backwater for tax purposes, but was immediately put off following a horrifying incident involving a Manx cat – a genetically impaired mutant that is somewhat indicative of the rest of the island's inhabitants.

10. BELGRADE

I don't think I've ever been to a place where people urinate in public as much as they do in Belgrade. Not an enjoyable experience when you don't own any shoes.

9. MEXICO CITY

A smog-filled, traffic-clogged featureless sprawl of concrete – all the wonderful things I look for in a city. If you're lucky you'll get kidnapped (or catnapped) by one of the cartels.

8. AMSTERDAM

Whilst on the surface Amsterdam appears to be reasonably pleasant, scratch beneath that and you'll find a city beset by tulips, windmills and bicycles. Ghastly.

7. SLOUGH

If only someone had heeded Sir John Betjeman's request when he wrote: 'Come, friendly bombs, and fall on Slough.' I've never been to such a godforsaken, foul-smelling and desolate place in all my days. The people look utterly miserable, and well they should. Even the birdsong is depressing. The anus of the western world.

6. BUCHAREST

I would honestly rather holiday in the Darfur region than go back there again. Full of emaciated peasants whose language is nonsensical and whose currency is the turnip, its most popular delicacy is something akin to the common earthworm. Bring your own food.

5. TOKYO

Aside from the sweltering humidity and general overcrowding, I don't take kindly to being stopped and searched by the police for no good reason. It was just as well that I left the blueprints for the Senshu Bank in my hotel room.

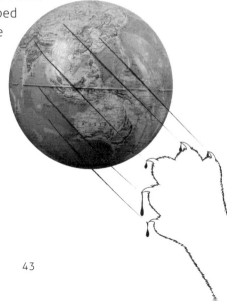

4. TOBRUK

To say that I felt about as safe in Tobruk as a Yorkshire terrier in a Chinese butchers would be a gross understatement. Avoid like the proverbial plague, unless you have a taste for mindless thuggery or an inclination for contracting diseases that have been elsewhere extinct for two centuries. Such as the proverbial plague.

3. RIGA

Riga was always a bleak and unfriendly place before it became the destination of choice for repulsive buffoons on their economy stag dos. Throw in these clusters of inebriated clowns in giant penis outfits and you're left with a city that at best resembles a drunkards' crèche.

2. SHANGHAI

Delightful city. Lord knows what the pollution did to my lungs, but witnessing first-hand the locals' partiality for sleeping with their poultry gave me a better understanding of how and why avian flu became so virulent.

1. SIDMOUTH

Surely a quaint little fishing town on the Devonshire coast wouldn't make it near this list, let alone reach the dreaded number 1 spot? Wrong. It's everything I despise in a place – coaches of half-dead elderly tourists, cream teas, donkey sanctuaries, disgruntled locals, model railways, the lingering stench of rotten fish and overpriced hotels that have seen better days. Congratulations, Sidmouth!

CONCEPTUAL ART

The fact that I could realistically open an award-winning conceptual art exhibition featuring me defecating into a collection of vintage headwear and call it 'The Cat Shat in a Hat', tells me all I need to know about this trite medium. It is as pretentious as it is preposterous. What Monet, Van Gogh, Picasso, Rembrandt and Dali would think of a fetid, hirsute tree-hugger exhibiting their unmade bed and its accompanying detritus is anyone's guess. My hope is that they would make it. And then paint it.

POLITICS

I don't mind admitting it, but I dearly miss the muscle flexing, the posturing and the downright stubbornness of the Cold War. It was a golden era for me personally, not least because I was an integral cog in a machine that created outlandish schemes to play the East and West off against each other. My, how we virile young bucks howled with laughter as they came perilously close to nuclear war – those truly were wonderful times.

Opportunity for derivative high street coffee shop chair

I'd give my back left paw to be sitting in the orangery at the old Parisian HQ again, drinking Rémy Martin with my dear friend and colleague Number 5 over a game of chess, and drawing up schematics for a fully operational volcano lair (right) from which we would carry out our plans for world domination.

Alas, nowadays politicians are so totally bereft of personality, imagination and wit. Instead they resemble a bunch of hapless toads squabbling over the tedious minutiae of something entirely futile. At least in the latter half of the twentieth century they didn't mind getting their hands dirty. They were also punctual when it came to paying ransoms.

SITCOMS

As an ardent fan of the classic British sitcom, I decided to have a go at writing my own – something I have long dreamed of doing but was never able to because of work commitments. *Beware of the Cat* is a semi-autobiographical black comedy (they always say you should write what you know). However, the feedback I received from Bruised Sky Productions following my submission wasn't exactly what I was hoping for. The bastards.

TITLE	BEWARE OF THE CAT		
DIRECTOR	BLOFELD'S CAT		
CAMERA			
DATE	SCENE	TAKE	
	3	5	

BRUISED SKY PRODUCTIONS LTD.

Tuesday, 24 March 2015

Dear Mr Cat,

Thank you for submitting your treatment and pilot script for *Beware of the Cat* into our new ventures programme for aspiring writers. Please accept my apologies for the delayed response, but as you can imagine we received hundreds of submissions, all of which needed our careful consideration.

Having now had a chance to review your pitch, I'm afraid we won't be taking it on and developing it further. Whilst we thought the premise was unquestionably different, the overtly mean-spirited and psychotic character traits of the protagonist didn't sit comfortably with the panel, neither did your declaration that '*Beware of the Cat* is a sitcom for the whole family, in the vein of *Fawlty Towers* and *The Good Life*'. To be honest, we found no part of your submission comparable to these iconic programmes, nor did we find any humour whatsoever in reading about a drug-addled cat ram-raiding a charity shop in a stolen Honda Civic. It is certainly not something that I would let my 4-year-old son watch.

Likewise, we thought the relationship between the protagonist and his 'gauche, megalomaniacal owner' to be clumsy and at times bizarre, as was the language, which was both crude and offensive to several ethnic groups. I ought to point out that the term 'black comedy' should not be used as a reference to the colour of one's skin. We also found the frequent sexual inferences to be unnecessary and rather vulgar.

I hope this doesn't discourage you from continuing to write, but we would urge a clearer understanding between what you are writing and who you consider to be your target audience.

I wish you the best of luck for the future.

Yours sincerely,

Eunice Draper
Head of Development
Bruised Sky Productions Ltd

HALLOWEEN

I think it's fair to say that the *raison d'être* of Halloween has been lost amidst the flurry of increasingly peculiar and elaborate costumes. At its heart it's nothing more than an evening in which parents encourage their repellent offspring, already foaming at the mouths due to their insatiable thirst for E numbers, to beg for more sugar. I recall one particular Halloween when we had several of the local degenerates descend on HQ. We entered into the spirit of the season by releasing the hounds, thus giving them a proper fright.

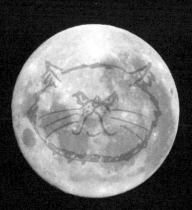

PUBLIC TRANSPORT

Two words that chill the blood and send waves of terror right through me. Aside from the underground monorail, which I've always found to be a rather pleasant way of getting around (hence its installation at HQ), my general opinion on riding public transport is not favourable.

Were it not for the fractured pelvis I sustained in 2009 after coming off second best in a fight with a Ford Fiesta, I can say in all honesty that I would never have had the misfortune of having to travel on the bus. The musty concoction of urine, body odour and fast food blended together to form the aroma of a tramp's yeast infection, and having to make polite small talk with an elderly spinster about how her geraniums had taken a beating from the recent inclement weather wasn't something that came easily to me. It's certainly not an experience I will endure again – fractured pelvis or not.

GAME SHOW CONTESTANTS

When Jean-Paul Sartre famously wrote that 'Hell is other people', he must have had the game show contestant in mind. Indeed, the contestant, more often than not called Sharon, is a most objectionable specimen. Whenever I've had the misfortune of watching a game show, Sharon's ability to chat inanely with the equally insufferable presenter renders me apoplectic. No one cares about your atrocious family, Sharon. And as for her incessantly cheerful disposition, even when she bungles the simplest of questions and misses out on a fortune? Well, it makes me want to claw at her stupid, plump face. 'Sorry, Sharon, you've just squandered the chance to win £1,000,000. Poor little Johnny's medical fees will have to go unpaid. Jolly bad luck.' Give them hell, Sharon – don't just accept it and wave to the camera, grinning like a halfwit. Take hostages, maul the presenter, vomit on the audience, *do something*!

THE HORSEMEAT SCANDAL

I found the recent horsemeat scandal in the UK something of an oddity. Quite why it enjoyed such a prolonged period of pre-eminence in the press is beyond me. It's baffling that those inclined to purchase near zero-cost frozen ready meals were then horrified by the quality of the meat they were consuming. What did they expect, assurances that their 99p lasagne consisted of only finely cut, mature-aged Wagyu beef? They should lace the next batch with arsenic as an effective measure for population control. What a shame I never ran for public office.

FINE DINING

Following last week's humiliating episode when I got stuck in my cat flap, my private veterinarian has just informed me that I am the first cat in history to be diagnosed with gout. Consequently, I will have to make some serious nutritional concessions, such as being weaned off the caviar, fois gras, potted ham and vintage wine, and forced on to a wretched diet of steamed haddock and milk. Suppertime will no doubt become something of a burden, but my mobility and night vision should improve tenfold – although I'm sure I'll still be more inclined to pick off the local mice with my shotgun rather than chase after the little blighters.

CONTEMPORARY MUSIC

Not all contemporary music is abhorrent bilge. There are one or two artists today who can hold a tune (Engelbert Humperdinck and Diana Ross, for example), and we've recently begun to inflict something called 'dubstep' on prisoners at HQ as a method of torture, providing most satisfactory results. But there is nothing more sickening in the world of music than the 'boy band'. It's a maddeningly puerile phenomenon I've never come to terms with, made worse by the ceaseless teenage, knicker-wetting hysteria that seems to accompany it. When adults understandably bemoan the many failings of today's youth, they should look no further than the deifying of these vacuous, vaginal discharges, with their foppish hair, sterile personalities and their overweening sense of entitlement. How anyone can listen to their adolescent vapourings and not want to gun down a flock of defenceless sheep is mystifying.

HUMAN RESOURCES

The charmless jobsworths of the Human Resources department, the Achilles' heel of any cutting-edge enterprise, have been a thorn in the side of all global extortion organisations in recent times. Gone are the halcyon days when one could simply throw a useless member of staff to the piranhas without having to enter it into the 'accident' book (incidentally, the 'P' in P45 always used to stand for piranhas). Nowadays, not only are there the boorish unions to contend with, but also appraisals and performance reviews: 'Let's sit down over a cup of coffee and chat about where you see yourself in two years' time,' etc. What utter bunkum! Whilst I like to think we offer generous remuneration and a healthy benefits package to all new employees, poor performance is still greeted with dismissal – both from work and from life.* I just don't tell anyone in HR.

*Whether or not they read the small print in their contracts is not my problem.

DOGS

Filthy bitches! I should preface this little musing by saying that any creature that eats its own excrement and greets others by sniffing their rectums has no place in civilised (or uncivilised) society. It is a cause of permanent bewilderment to me that mankind not only allows these flea-ridden, foul smelling,

dim-witted, violent and greedy animals into their homes, but also treats them like family. What's even more peculiar is that there are heathens on this planet who actually eat these vile specimens – surely not even a mongrel would stomach such contemptible cuisine (notwithstanding a 'dog-eat-dog' scenario, of course)?

BUDGET AIRLINES

Circumstances recently conspired against me and I was forced to fly with a budget airline. Having been accustomed to first-class air travel for much of my life, to say that this was amongst the most intolerable experiences I've ever had to withstand is a wild understatement. I was in a state of high dudgeon when I was forced, against my will, to take a seat next to what can only be described as a human hippopotamus. I took up little of my pew, which was just as well as my behemoth of a neighbour was spilling out across much of the aisle, consuming everything (including me) beneath his fleshy blanket of a stomach. Why this perspiring Godzilla was allowed to travel in the first place is beyond me, but when you consider this alongside the vomit-inducing food on offer, the barefaced insolence of the air stewards, the derisory lack of luggage space and the negligible flying skills of the 'pilot' (whose landing was akin to being plucked from the sky and hurled towards the ground), I think it's fair to say that I shan't be a repeat customer. Below is a note I received from the lickspittle that are Air-2-Air airlines (missiles?) following my letter of complaint.

AIR-2-AIR

Dear Mr Cat,

Re: Flight A2AXY346 – AKA the Flight from the Bowels of Hell

Thank you for taking the time to inform us of your misgivings regarding your recent flight on Air-2-Air airlines from London Gatwick to Nice. I have looked into your complaints and would like to address them in this letter. Firstly, your claim that you were 'repeatedly groped by several members of the incompetent cabin crew' is at odds with their version of events. Upon speaking with the crew in question, they said that they had never seen anyone consume so much alcohol on a two-hour flight, least of all a cat, and were repeatedly called upon to restrain you from verbally and physically abusing your fellow passengers and rebuff your belligerent demands that *Columbo* be screened as the in-flight entertainment. Secondly, your thoughts that 'the pilot must have terrorist sympathies, as it's the only thing that can explain his willingness to crash the aeroplane upon landing' are both wildly inaccurate and highly offensive, as is your suggestion that we should 'ban obese people from [our] aeroplanes'. Our service is for all, irrespective of age, gender, colour, height or weight. Finally, your remarks that 'even the Borrowers would've experienced difficulty in traversing the overhead lockers, such was the lack of space' and 'the food at best resembled Labrador sputum' are as patently ridiculous as they are ignorant. I wholeheartedly suggest that you travel with our competitors in the future if you believe our service to be 'embarrassingly bungling from start to finish'.

Yours sincerely,

Tim Bray
Customer Service Manager
Air-2-Air

COMMERCIAL SPACE FLIGHT

I don't feel particularly comfortable with the idea that the unspeakably vile nouveau riche will soon be able to enjoy a scenic but otherwise exorbitant trip into outer space. I was much happier when the planet's purlieu was the domain of only the superpowers, to be contested like an astrological chessboard. So much for the final frontier ... unless, of course, the plan is to jettison these bourgeois abominations into space and leave them marooned amongst the stars?

TABLOIDS

I have never been to a country that enjoys the gutter press more than the UK. Quite why the general public takes such delight in the frivolous drivel spouted by these slippery underlings masquerading as journalists is indeed a vexing conundrum.

Personally, I like my newspaper to provide me with a veneer of impartiality, as well as a factually correct update on current affairs (both domestic and worldwide). I certainly do not care to see the following stories on the front page of any rag, no matter how cheap and tasteless the publication is:

🐾 **A glorified weather report on how biblical floods are going to decimate small towns and villages across the land, leaving us open to the possibility that by 2200 the human race will have developed gills**

🐾 **How an irascible footballer has spent a small fortune on high-class prostitutes, cocaine and online bingo**

🐾 **Outlandish claims that the UK is to be invaded by thousands of diseased immigrants intent on raping** and pillaging, and repaving driveways all over the country

- That consuming two glasses of vintage claret a day will leave you at a 90 per cent risk of developing dementia (in which case, from henceforth, I'd better start wearing a name badge and labelling everything)

- How Natalie from Nuneaton has spent £25,000 on enlarging her bust to resemble two hot-air balloons. This is not news. It is an advert for self-inflation

EMAIL

I long for the days when my working lunch consisted of a three-course meal at Le Grand Véfour, ably accompanied by a silky Cahors, before I disappeared to the Palais Garnier for the afternoon, safe in the knowledge that I wouldn't have to return to HQ squiffy (with my tail literally between my legs) and follow up on the countless mercy letters from the politicians we'd blackmailed.

Sadly times have changed, and the incessant desire for frequent communication and the need to know of one's whereabouts have made these delightful little sojourns a thing of the past. However, in defence of modern working practice, email communication has improved productivity tenfold and has certainly made the world a smaller place. This point was emphasised recently when I discovered, to my genuine surprise, that I had won the Nigerian National Lottery on two separate occasions. Thanks to the wonderfully detailed emails from one Derek Ajobole, all that was required from me were my bank account details and passwords. Firstly, how imbecilic does Derek think I am? And secondly, does he know who I work for?

Derek, if you're reading this and looking to get a proper job, this is not the best way to put yourself in the shop window. Alas, you will never know.

THE ELDERLY

Age catches up with us all eventually, so I should choose my words here carefully. When one begins to smell of lavender and boiled sweets, loses the ability to drive above 40mph and starts bleating on about how 'this never happened in my day', you know it's time to be put out to pasture or dispatched to the nearest glue factory. Whilst I do retain some sympathy for society's octogenarians, I do find their persistent mollycoddling infuriating. I often wonder how our geriatric friends would react if I were to continually pat them on their wizened heads, insist on stroking their lank, dusty hair, and force-feed them tins of regurgitated pig shit.

Even Number 1 has begun to display worrying signs of becoming long in the tooth. Not only has he started to have issues with his bladder control (much to my chagrin when he insists that I sit on his lap), he also appears to have forgotten some rather alarming details in recent years, such as where in Iraq he left those WMDs. You may have read about these?

SUPERMARKETS

Ugh. Where does one begin? I would rather cough up a pumpkin-sized hairball than coax a broken shopping trolley around a soulless, artificially lit warehouse of battery-farmed animal carcasses again. Gangs of combative mothers, silver-haired malcontents, feral children and drunken hoodlums roam the aisles, vying for what's left of the 'special offers' – more often than not comprised of inedible 'ready meals' (apparently there is also a budget range?!) and wine that has thrice passed through the urinary tract of a rabid badger. And if you survive this distressing experience, one is then greeted by the mile-long queues at the checkouts – conveyor belts operated by middle-aged womenfolk who would rather gossip with their portly colleagues than serve the thousands of shoppers waiting patiently to reacquaint themselves with the outside world. Of course, you always have the option of using the self-service machines, but given the fact that you require a PhD in Astrophysics to operate these infernal contraptions, you're best advised to wait for Maureen to finish nattering with Mavis about Muriel's husband's erectile dysfunction. Horrendous from start to finish.

CATNIP

My addiction to catnip and, ultimately, 'meow meow' first became problematic during our tenure at the isolated HQ in the Swiss Alps. I've never had a head for heights and I'm rather ambivalent towards cold weather, so in order to abide this rather sorry period I turned to catnip – vast quantities of it, in fact. I had plenty of money and spare time, and there was a dealer residing in a neighbouring village whose 'nip' was as pure as the snow that covered the nearby mountains and had me purring like a Geiger counter. It was the perfect storm, if you will. Overnight I turned from a dour, narcissistic and malicious cat into something worse. It all culminated in me garrotting a representative of an injury lawyers firm, who was seeking damages on behalf of a former employee involved in a skiing accident. Which leads me conveniently on to …

INJURY LAWYERS

HURT & SCARED INJURY LAWYERS

To Whom It May Concern

Re: The injuries sustained by Mr Heinrich Schmitz

As the legal representatives of the above-mentioned Mr Schmitz, a junior weapons technician within your organisation, we are writing to inform you that we will be seeking damages for the injuries sustained by our client during a recent high-speed ski chase. An independent doctor has verified Mr Schmitz's injuries as:

Broken fibula in the left leg
Torn medial ligaments in the right knee and right ankle
Memory loss and trauma
Eczema

We will, of course, keep you informed as to how we wish to proceed in the coming weeks.

Yours sincerely,

Richard Hallam (TUCN)
Solicitor
Hurt & Scared Injury Lawyers

Dear Mr Hallam,

Re: The injuries sustained by Mr Heinrich 'I couldn't ski if I had a gun held to my head' Schmitz

Many thanks for your recent letter — not least because it provided our *capable* staff with some much-needed hilarity. Mr Schmitz is widely considered to be one of the most hopelessly inept individuals we have ever employed, and despite our continued efforts to help improve his skiing he persists in showing about as much flair as a disabled rhinoceros on roller skates. You mentioned in your letter that Mr Schmitz had developed 'memory loss and trauma' following the accident. This would indeed be a medical first, as Mr Schmitz's mental capabilities prior to his mishap were negligible at best (you can't lose something you don't have, etc.). We eagerly await your future missives, if indeed they deliver as much amusement as your first.

Yours, in haste,

Blofeld's Cat (CAT)
Head of Operations

Dear Mr Cat,

Re: The injuries sustained by Mr Heinrich Schmitz

Shortly after I received your contemptible reply to my perfectly reasonable letter, the body of Mr Schmitz arrived by first-class courier at our offices. He was attached to a pair of skis. Needless to say, this has not only caused untold stress to our staff members here but also to Mr Schmitz's family. The horrific injuries suffered by Mr Schmitz seem to be consistent with multiple piranha bites, and, as such, I have informed the relevant authorities, who will no doubt be investigating this further (piranhas aren't native to Switzerland after all!). I will also be visiting you in person at the earliest possible opportunity to discuss a settlement with Mr Schmitz's family. Yours is a despicable organisation, and I look forward to the day when we no longer have to tolerate your underhand scare tactics and oppression.

Yours sincerely,

Richard Hallam (TUCN)
Solicitor
Hurt & Scared Injury Lawyers

Dear Mr Hallam,

Re: The injuries sustained by Mr Heinrich Schmitz

One can only hope that Mr Schmitz's journey to the pearly gates didn't require him to ski.

Up yours,

Blofeld's Cat (MEOW)
Head of Operations

Me and my family. I abhorred every minute I spent with the insufferable tribe and couldn't wait to leave them.

When I first ventured out on my own, I spent Christmas with this man ('Mad' Jean-Pierre) and his menagerie of revolting canines. I learned how to survive Paris' mean streets and became a killer stray with a fearsome reputation. (Natalie HG)

An oil rig similar to the one we once called home. We don't talk about this particular era anymore. (Ken Hodge)

Our HQ in Switzerland. Whilst Number 1 loved the Alps and enjoyed nothing more than creating snow angels, I became reliant on artificial stimulants to get me through the long winter evenings. (ActiveSteve)

Our new, improved volcano lair. Broadband is still a bit temperamental, however. (Vincent)

Jamal, one of my pet Siamese fighting fish. He was a gift from Number 1 following my first promotion. Sadly, he didn't last long as I was hungry one afternoon. (Michelle Tribe)

Nosferatu, King Herod, Mungo, Gottfried, Pascal, Lemuel, The Duke of Bedford and the rest of the gang: the first piranhas we had at HQ. They were exceptionally hardworking and most amusing. Unfortunately, we had to let go of Nosferatu and Mungo following an incident at a Christmas party. (Pete)

Amelie, our latest recruit. No longer will staff phone me to say that they can't come into work because of something suspect they ate the previous evening. (Elias Levy)

Napoleon, my arch-nemesis. Can't abide the mongrel. (Tim Dawson)

Sidmouth. Sounds horrible, and is. (Ian Stedman)

King Richard III of England would've made an excellent operative at HQ, hunchback and all.

Disco fever. I was often found tearing up the dance floors of Parisian nightclubs during the heady disco days of the 1970s.

TATTOOS

The only explanation I can think of for why certain individuals choose to blemish their skin with permanent ink is that they are absent-minded. Why else would anyone willingly submit to the pain of having all seven of their children's names (a derivative of a white wine grape) and dates of birth forever etched on to their bloated torsos in some garish calligraphy? It'll be shopping lists and passwords next.

6 PEOPLE FROM HISTORY WHO WOULD'VE MADE PERFECT OPERATIVES AT HQ

1. RICHARD III

Aside from being afflicted by a physical deformity (which is actually something of a prerequisite for our chief operatives), Dick III had the nerve to hold his two nephews captive whilst he went about securing his crown, and ought to be lauded.

2. NAPOLEON BONAPARTE

Fiercely intelligent and totally merciless, Napoleon's unrivalled lust for power and thirst for conquest would've made him an ideal leadership candidate. Just don't mention his height.

3. KIM JONG-IL

Completely despotic and indisputably unhinged, Kim Jong-il even looked the part in his buttoned-up Nehru jacket and NHS spectacles. He also possessed unrivalled powers of persuasion, having convinced his countrymen that he shot no less than eleven holes-in-one on his first ever round of golf. He must've thought twelve was stretching a point?

4. VLAD THE IMPALER

Perhaps more suited to the role of henchman rather than operative due to his mental instability, Vlad made a name for himself in fifteenth-century Transylvania for extraordinary sadism when he skewered thousands of Turks on their own kebabs. See also: Ivan the Terrible and Attila the Hun.

5. EDWARD LONGSHANKS

The Machiavellian monarch was a ruthless ruler as well as a scheming and brilliant tactician, whose ability with the sword was unmatched by any of his predecessors. Whilst I'm certain he would've approved of our operations, he would certainly not have approved of Scottish independence.

6. LUCREZIA BORGIA

The ultimate femme fatale and a prominent member of the suitably reptilian and power-hungry House of Borgia (infamous for adultery, theft, simony and bribery during the Italian Renaissance), Lucrezia was particularly adept at poisoning her enemies with arsenic. What she lacked as a hostess she made up for in sheer treachery.

ASTROLOGY

Astrologers are an unusual breed, yet I can't help but admire them for the way they've managed to convince millions of cretins to hang on their every word as if their pathetic lives depended on it. These flatulent eccentrics are con artists, and poor ones at that. To solidify my argument, my daily horoscope reads thus:

★★★★★★★★★★★★★★★★★★★★★★★★★★★★★★

It's the little things that make you wonder what's just around the corner – all the details seem to point toward something big! Now is the time to focus on the small things and be prepared when the big stuff comes.'

★★★★★★★★★★★★★★★★★★★★★★★★★★★★★★

What does this even mean?! That I should don some sort of body armour and expect to be struck by a train? Absolute gibberish.

MY IDEAL DINNER PARTY

I have agonised over this list, as it's a question I've often been asked. I eventually settled on the six below, the perfect number for any salubrious dinner party.

🐾 Me, obviously.

🐾 Barry Manilow, who would not only offer delightful company but also an enchanting musical interlude in between courses.

- 🐾 Bette Davis, whose fiery temperament and independent spirit would undoubtedly make for splendid conversation.

- 🐾 David Niven, whose charm and taste for the finer things in life would bring an air of sophistication to the proceedings.

- 🐾 Mata Hari – courtesan, spy, exotic dancer, the ultimate dinner party guest. Just make sure you lock up the family silver ...

- 🐾 Kaiser Wilhelm, whose bombastic and mercurial personality would guarantee an unpredictable evening.

SELFIES

Anyone caught taking a 'selfie' (surely the hoi polloi should know what they look like by now?!) should be automatically posted to the nearest penal colony* to serve a life sentence.

*These still exist, right?

MISERY MEMOIRS

Does your book have a picture of an ashen-faced child looking absolutely crestfallen on the front cover and a one-word title that is typically a synonym of the word 'Broken'? Then the chances are you're reading a 'misery memoir', the genre of choice for overweight, unemployable single mothers residing in high-rise tenements. I'm not sure which group is worse – the wretches who peddle this tripe or the philistines who take great pleasure in reading (should they have the aptitude) these trashy biographies of childhood abuse and neglect. I wouldn't ordinarily advocate book burning, but in this instance I'll make an exception. Either that or I recommend you read it to your captives to make them even more miserable.

VEGETARIANS

Aside from teetotallers (at least those who've made a lifestyle choice not to drink), there is only one group of people I wholeheartedly object to and it's militant vegetarians. I simply cannot fathom why anyone not under duress would readily order lentil soup as a main course, or quite why they would forego a hearty beef stroganoff in lieu of a potato salad. How these undernourished hipsters in their skinny jeans have the strength to stand, let alone walk, is a mystery to me. Animals are supposed to be eaten – as per the food chain – and this is coming from a cat who has made a habit of circumnavigating backstreet Asian butchers as if his life quite literally depended on it.

THE EUROVISION SONG CONTEST

I would sooner boil my genitals in vinegar or burn one of my nine lives than watch these obscene novelty acts parade about the stage like the herd of abominable exhibitionists they are. My repeated request that we should host this carnival of the bizarre at HQ has been continually denied by the contest's organisers. Perhaps they are wise to my plan that would see us kidnap the acts and use them as live targets for our operatives? We would certainly be doing Europe a favour: the fewer death metal bands clad in bondage leather and transgender divas flaunting their wares the better. Nul points indeed!

THE VETS

A visit to the vets is a consistently degrading undertaking for any cat (or domesticated animal for that matter). To this day I'm still not sure why Number 1 insists on having me wormed – it's not as if I've ever come bounding through my cat flap looking for approval with a malodorous piece of roadkill wedged in my mouth. But it's the humiliating experience of having one's temperature taken that is the epitome of veterinary indignity. A simple procedure, I hear you say? Well it would be if it were administered orally. Sadly, these vile perverts insist otherwise.

VALENTINE'S DAY

Words fail to do justice to the odium I have for this farcical ritual. As a confirmed bachelor, it is always a considerable inconvenience to find my favourite restaurants occupied by courting couples dribbling all over each other, whilst I have to suffer the ignominy of having this nauseating charade forced upon me. I remember on one occasion being serenaded by a musical trio as I dined alone, much to the amusement of the lovebirds sitting on the table next to me. They didn't find it quite so amusing when I had the young gentleman's heart presented to his lady friend in a ramekin.

TELEVISION TALENT SHOWS

Christ in a handbasket, haven't we endured these contrived atrocities (controcities?) for long enough?! The irony that a 'celebrity' who is famous for being married to someone with actual talent and an antiquated singer who has made a career out of murdering classic songs are now earning a living from judging the ability of others is unbearable. Not quite as unbearable as the mandatory 'sob stories' from the talent(less) show contestants themselves, though. I have no interest in the fact that rotund Simon, 23, from Boston is appearing on the show because his mother's ravenous appetite for sugary drinks and doughnuts has left her incapacitated with type 2 diabetes, nor that warbling Crystal, 28, from Croydon needs to win to feed the mouths of her twelve bastard children. Get a proper job and never darken my television again, you appalling monstrosities!

DIY

Having recently volunteered to oversee the refurbishment at HQ (a job that I assumed would be relatively straightforward), I can unequivocally say that, aside from emptying Number 1's colostomy bag with untrimmed claws, this has to rank up there as one of the most excruciating tasks I've ever undertaken.

Foolishly assuming that purchasing six tins of red matt emulsion paint would be a simple assignment, the pugnacious salesman proceeded to introduce me to thirty-nine different hues, from 'Autumn Blaze' to 'Tuscan Sunset', and thus gave me a true understanding of what it's like to feel one's life slipping away. The conversation came to an abrupt end when I threatened to daub my office in a shade called 'Salesman's Blood'.

But agonising over paint colours paled into insignificance when it came to assembling the new office furniture. If I'm ever lucky enough to hunt down the gargantuan imbecile who designed these ill-fitting wooden demons, I'll have him fastened to his desk with the nails that wouldn't fit into our half-assembled shelves. You, sir, are a rapscallion of the highest order, and your instructions are about as helpful as a plaster for the gunshot wound you will shortly be receiving.

FAST-FOOD RESTAURANTS

If your gastronomy of choice is a congealed beef patty consisting of the minced scrotum of a rheumatic bull sandwiched between a sweaty bap, and your preferred clientele are screaming children, negligent parents and monosyllabic adolescents, then this is the place for you. Be warned though: these are not restaurants. Nor do they serve food. And for the most part they're not very fast. The staff are always a delight, though.

CAT FOOD

I hold nothing but complete disdain for companies that package their cat 'food' (and I use that word in the loosest sense possible) in either a sachet, a tin, or a large bag that looks as if it should be filled with compost. My latest complaint (below), written a whole three months ago to the detestable dullards at 'Feline Fancies', has been shamefully ignored. Unfortunately for them, my next line of communication will not be a written one.

Dear Cretins,

Re: Feline Fancies' 'Tasty Treats' range

Having previously written to you on 21 October 2012 after suffering a bout of appalling acid indigestion from consuming one of your 'Mature Moggy Delights Beef and Tomato' dinners, I find it rather astonishing to be writing to you yet again, this time regarding the violent diarrhoea (a sample enclosed) your 'Luscious Lamb and Carrots' dish delightfully provided me with during a recent social engagement.

The swill that you market under the slogan 'delicious food for the senior cat' is clearly in breach of the Trade Descriptions Act. It has patently never seen a lamb (or even a carrot) in its miserable existence, and I am left in no doubt that this gelatinous mound of beige matter consists of nothing more than the rectal shavings of a cumbersome pig.

May I suggest launching a connoisseurs range, perhaps a Filet Mignon or an Aylesbury duck (made with actual beef and duck)? Price is not an issue here, but the arrogance with which you treat your customers is.

I eagerly await your obsequious response.

Yours sincerely,

Blofeld's Cat

MUSICALS

3 September, 1996. A date forever etched in my memory. Number 1 thought it would be a wonderful idea for the two of us to take a day trip to London's glittering West End, which in theory was a splendid plan, yet proved to be an unmitigated disaster.

The day started well enough: a delightful stroll through Regent's Park in the late summer sun was followed by a sumptuous dinner at The Criterion (the pan-fried monkfish being the real showstopper). Sadly, this was to be the final highlight as the day rapidly descended into chaos.

I should say that having endured *Les Misérables* a few years earlier (seven hours of my life I'll never get back), I was naturally anxious that watching a cast of jobbing actors inexplicably bursting into song whilst pretending to be cats (in the imaginatively titled musical *Cats*) would leave me baying for blood. Yet Number 1 insisted it would be fun, and who was I to disagree? However, within the first five minutes my suspicions were confirmed. The direction was lamentable, the storyline an incoherent mess, and the acting on par with that of a village am-dram production of *Mother Goose*.

To this day I'm still uncertain what happened next but, with my rage already at boiling point after suffering 'Jellicle Songs for Jellicle Cats', by the time Old Deuteronomy had entered this sickening farce I found myself up on stage, viciously assaulting several innocuous chorus members, before clawing my way towards Munkustrap and Old Deuteronomy himself. I could see Number 1 looking on in horror, but it was too late. By now I had attacked half of the cast, whilst the other half desperately tried to restrain me.

I have no major regrets over what transpired that fateful day, and in retrospect I believe the cast were given an invaluable tutorial in what a genuinely irate and borderline drunk cat behaves like. My only slight compunction is that Number 1 spent a considerable sum on my bail application, facial reconstructive surgery for Mungojerrie, and bribing the press to withhold the story from the papers and the judge to keep my sentence down to only fifty hours of community service. My request to give the cast further acting tutorials as opposed to picking up litter in Isleworth was rejected out of hand.

Postscript: I politely declined a recent invitation to see *The Lion King*.

SPORT

I'm quite happy to admit that, with the notable exceptions of conceptual art, musical theatre and the loathsome pantomime, I've always had a preference for the arts over watching groups of over-aroused ruffians chasing a pig's bladder around a muddy field – even though joining the tribes of lobotomised fans in chanting obscenities at the referee can be rather jolly. But having to feign interest in a certain round ball event every four years because Number 1 is a silent partner to the sport's governing body is undoubtedly a challenge – although, having said that, organising the bidding process for one of their upcoming tournaments did provide me with a frisson of excitement.

CELEBRITY CULTURE

Since when did Stacey from Newcastle, a girl infamous for being orange, exposing her genitals and vomiting in public become a 'celebrity'? I long for the days of watching Dusty Springfield, Marcel Marceau and Rudolph Nureyev exhibit their genuine talents in public. Yet these days, for some ungodly reason, thousands of idiots tune in each week to watch dear old Stacey and her miscreant pals in their own television show – a show in which they copulate on cue, have their vaginas tattooed and binge drink until they pass out.

If I had my way, I'd have them rounded up at gunpoint and dropped near a military base in North Korea, thus safeguarding their celebrity status by making them more famous in death than in life. It would certainly make for more interesting television.

NIGHTCLUBS

Once upon a time a nightclub was full of bonhomie and packed with upstanding merrymakers who could actually dance. Regrettably, the modern-day discothèque seems to have attracted quite the opposite clientele. Every weekend, these repugnant revellers, dressed as if clothes rationing is still enforced, converge upon a collection of damp, dimly lit crucibles of crime to fight and fornicate with other like-minded souls. One can only surmise that these dens of iniquity have been ironically christened with utopic names such as Eden, Heaven and Paradise.

Upon arrival, the revellers are afforded the same welcome as the one Columbus no doubt received from the natives on his maiden voyage to the Americas, except in this instance the natives are the bouncers – typically heavy-set cavemen in cheap suits. If you're (un)lucky enough to have been granted entry by one of these neckless gorillas, you're then free to either engage in a bout of pugilism with a kebab-stained thug (Queensbury rules are not applicable), sexually assault a drunken strumpet, or attempt to dance to music that sounds as if it's been recorded in a blacksmith's workshop. Paradise, indeed.

CINEMA

There was a time when a pilgrimage to the cinema was my favourite pursuit. The silver screen, as it was once known, was one of life's great pleasures. Now it's just home to hackneyed drivel. Sound and colour have been two pivotal developments in the history of movie making, and contemporary filmmakers seem compelled to honour both by farting out as much of each as they can, almost as if it's a competition. Subsequently, a trip to the cinema today amounts to nothing more than two hours of sensory abuse, made worse by the ridiculous, over-sized plastic goggles you're often cajoled into wearing. Indeed, experiencing the full assault of 3D cinema is an altogether more exhausting undertaking in which you're aurally and visually battered with all the delicacy of a jackhammer to the temple.

And it gets worse! As is progressively the case in the modern world, any vestiges of proper etiquette and decorum at the cinema have long since eroded. Today, the churlish chatter of the mindless masses you're forced to sit with invades the otherwise rare moments of aural reprieve, and if that's not enough you're probably sat next to some buffoon stuffing his acne-ridden face with grub that reeks of decomposition in between sending moronic text messages to his friend sat behind him. The other day someone even had the audacity to answer their phone! Where will it end? Well, for that particular movie-going patron it ended then in row H. With that in mind, whilst I've been advised not to name the cinema in question, I'd like to extend my thanks to the staff who were left to clean up a lot more than popcorn. FIN.

ESTATE AGENTS

I've been fortunate enough to have lived and worked in a number of extravagant properties over the years – it's one of the perks of being a criminal mastermind. But even criminal masterminds have to tolerate the severe inconvenience of dealing with the purveyors of misery that are estate agents when procuring property.

Even now as I write, my fur bristles at the thought of previous encounters with these servile scumbags, to say nothing of future encumbrances I shall no doubt endure. Their sickeningly fraudulent facades can never mask their true intentions of ripping you off at every opportunity, despite their glib insistences that they want what's best for you. I would ordinarily applaud such barefaced duplicity, but the inventory fees we incurred when we were forced out of our first volcano HQ were so outrageous that we had no option but to hunt down Messrs MacGeehan, Church & Doidge and put them out of business. Permanently.

REGIONAL DIALECTS

Having recently spent some time in the UK, I feel justified when I say that there is little to enjoy about this perpetually cold and bleak land. (One can only assume that Blake was being ironic when he wrote 'Jerusalem'.) The people are obnoxious, the food is bland and unexciting, the weather is excruciatingly miserable, and the claustrophobic, often squalid, living conditions make one want to invade one's neighbour's property all for the sake of a few extra square feet of living space.

And yet, despite this unendingly gloomy outlook, there are some interesting facets to old Britannia. The seemingly endless number of regional dialects and colloquialisms are of constant amusement to me. For example, if a crazed-looking man approached me, armed with an ice pick and a hardened Glaswegian brogue, I would stop preening myself and run for my life. However, if the same man were to speak with a soft Bristolian drawl I would merely laugh in his face over his penchant for dropping syllables and revel in the fact that he sounded like a pirate.

THE SEASIDE

'I do like to be beside the seaside,' went the popular British musical hall song, despite the fact that there is literally nothing pleasurable about being beside the seaside. Notwithstanding having to contend with the sand that somehow manages to invade every inch of your body, bathing in an amalgamation of glacial saltwater and human excretion does little for me, likewise having to share the beach with society's bottom feeders and their dreadful dogs. Whenever Number I demands a day spent beside the seaside, I pass the time by urinating on as many sandcastles as my bladder will permit me. Speaking of urine ...

TAP WATER

VOLCANH20

Dear Mr Cat,

Thank you for your recent letter highlighting your grievances with the water supplied by VolcanH20. We were very sorry to hear that our product hadn't met with satisfaction. However, I can assure you that you won't need to drink limescale remover to rid yourself of our 'chalky mildew', nor will you be 'bedridden with a hybrid of cholera, dysentery and typhoid'. I would also like to take this opportunity to point out that we have been consistently voted one of the best water providers in recent years, and your remark that 'even the dehydrated people of the third world would throw [our] puddles of rat piss back in the well' was met with astonishment in the office. We pride ourselves on the fact that our water is sourced directly from the volcanic mountains, despite your erroneous assertion that we take it in turns to empty ourselves into our consumers' pipes, so please do remember this the next time you take a sip of our 'tepid pond scum'.

I have sent one of our engineers out to your headquarters to perform a test on your water – however, he has gone missing. I will be in touch again once we locate him and receive the results of his findings.

Yours sincerely,

Ben Harris
Customer Care Manager
VolcanH20

ARMS DEALING

A noble profession.

PERSONAL GROOMING

Would someone care to explain to me why humans have become so obsessed with hair removal? There was a time when excess body hair was alluring. It would now appear that waxing or lasering every follicle from your body is de rigueur.

Being a dandy cat, it goes without saying that I'm rather fond of my luxuriant mane, and to that end I take my grooming very seriously. However, I can't make a trip to the chemists today without being overwhelmed by the many pheromone lotions, nipple resins, unicorn-vomit perfumes, bull-semen hair products, bird-poo facials, snail-goo moisturisers and placenta beauty products that are currently available. And what in the name of Beelzebub's ball bag is a styptic pencil?! A clean paw and a little spittle have always worked fine for me. Oh, and a splash of Drakkar Noir on special occasions.

ONLINE REVIEWS

One of the few advantages of the internet is that you're now free to condemn inadequate restaurants, abysmal tourist attractions and uninhabitable hotels for the world to see. Whilst most review for the benefit of others, as a habitual online critic I engage in spats with egregious hotel managers and pompous restaurateurs for my own personal amusement. The following is the war of words I became embroiled in with the manager of the Theodore Chester Hotel in Reading (situated in one of the town's less gentrified areas, if you can imagine such a thing). Should you ever find yourself marooned in Reading overnight, I'd recommend sleeping rough. It's certainly more comfortable and far less dangerous.

'*House of Horrors*'

⊙⊙⊙⊙⊙   Reviewed 8 July 2014

Having booked a night's stay at the Theodore Chester for a conference in June, my fellow delegates and I came away from our nightmarish visit feeling at once filthy, cheated, sleep-deprived, poisoned and violated. You may wonder what on earth could've transpired that fateful night to have left us all feeling so utterly bereaved. I shall endeavour to recount our traumatic experience as best I can so that you, dear reader, don't make the same fateful error.

Upon entering the Theodore Chester, we were immediately struck by the somewhat unique décor, which appeared to be emulating that of a multiple crime scene, and a receptionist who was graced with all the charm of a Nazi commandant. After a torturous 30-minute wait, we were finally acquainted with our room keys and made our way sheepishly to the lift. And when I say lift, I mean a rickety death shaft that had somehow evaded the scrutiny of the health and safety inspectors. Or had killed them.

Safely navigating this peril intact, I reticently entered my chamber, half expecting to discover a corpse in the bathroom. If only I had a bathroom! My quarters consisted of a solitary tobacco-stained room, little more than the size of a cupboard, in which a suspiciously discoloured mattress had been discarded in the corner, giving me the distinct impression that it had been recently used as a haven for crack whores. More on the communal bathroom later.

Deciding that we were peckish and having been informed that the local restaurants didn't amount to much, we were advised (against our better judgement) to enjoy a meal at the hotel's restaurant, Le Chat Brun – a name that would become painfully appropriate in time. The stout waitress, who in a former life would've made a formidable prop forward, shepherded us to our table as if it were a lifeboat on the *Titanic*. She proceeded to grunt her way through the specials board, pausing only for breath when asked a question, before discarding a collection of laminated menus (complete with a curious sticky residue) in front of her increasingly disconcerted customers. After perusing this frankly horrendous selection of care-home food, I plumped for the toad-in-the-hole, concluding that it was the dish least likely to kill me. I was wrong. The consistency of the sausage appeared to be that of actual toad, whilst the batter could've quite easily doubled as spackling paste. It certainly left a bad taste in the mouth and a rather nasty case of cat breath.

Somewhat predictably, it wasn't long before Mr Toad and the Polyfilla made their ignominious reappearance. I was woken in the middle of the night by the sound of thunder coming from within my room. Discovering that it was emitting from my stomach and foreseeing an imminent eruption, I thought it best to hobble to the bathroom and prepare myself for my own personal Pompeii. And then I was hit by the full realisation of the horror that awaited me. It was a communal toilet. Soon greeted by the sight of my colleagues, clearly in a similar state of distress and forming a not-so-orderly queue outside this cubicle of melancholy, I had no option but to brace myself before redecorating the walls of the corridor. Satisfied that I had fully exorcised my bowels, I returned to my room exhausted, embarrassed, corrupted and crestfallen.

I barely slept a wink that night. In between listening to the amateur porn stars re-enacting a scene from *Caligula* through the wafer-thin walls and my expelling the deaf cleaner (who had inexplicably taken it upon herself to enter my room uninvited on three separate occasions), by the time I finally drifted off I woke with a start to the sound of frantic hammering outside. Opening the door to the squat, cross-eyed hotel manager, he proceeded to lambast me and my colleagues for our 'shameful behaviour' and insisted we leave immediately. Not entirely convinced that English was his first (nor indeed his second) language, I attempted to reason with this chump and offered him an explanation for our actions, citing his toxic food as the catalyst for the devilry that had befallen us the previous night. It didn't work. We were forbidden from using the shared (prison?) shower facilities and, worse still, from enjoying a continental (incontinental?) breakfast at Le Chat Brun.

The rest of our stay was so forgettable I have forgotten it.

David Strike, Manager at the Theodore Chester Hotel, responded to this review, 9 July 2014

Dear Mr Cat,

Thank you for your review of our hotel and all its nauseating detail. If only it were an accurate reflection of what actually took place that night! I've consulted with those unfortunate enough to have been working on the day in question and they have informed me that you and your group were already riotously drunk by the time you arrived. Indeed, I gather from Myrtle, the waitress you so callously scolded in your review, that none of you actually ate in the restaurant as your food mostly ended up on the floor, the walls, the ceiling and even on your fellow diners.

As you will have seen on our website, your group pre-booked rooms without en-suite bathrooms at a very competitive rate, so why this came as a shock to you is a mystery. It certainly doesn't excuse your appalling rudeness towards me and my staff (Nazi goose-stepping around reception and holding the elderly cleaner hostage being the lowlights), nor does it justify your defecation contest on the second-floor corridor (which is still being redecorated, I hasten to add).

I sincerely hope future guests ignore your blatant distortion of the truth and instead read the many excellent reviews we have collected over the past year. As an accredited 3-star hotel, we always put our guests first. Apart from you, because you're banned.

David Strike
Manager
Theodore Chester Hotel, Reading

Blofeld's Cat replied to this response, 9 July 2014

Dear Mr Strike,

I am intrigued by your claim that you are 'an accredited 3-star hotel'. One wonders how this is classified and why the Guantanamo Bay detention camp has not been awarded the same certification.

I do apologise for my heartless description of the lantern-jawed Myrtle; however, you may want to double-check that she hasn't been eating the profits.

I would sooner romance a syphilitic skunk than return to your shambolic establishment.

Blofeld's Cat
Victim of the Theodore Chester Hotel, Reading

CAMPING

I make no bones about the fact that I very much enjoy my creature comforts. I am certainly not a cat prone to spending hours on end prowling about in the dark when I could be reclining in front of a roaring fire with a generous glass of Côte de Nuits in paw, which is why I found a recent camping excursion an unrelenting ordeal. Thoughtlessly agreeing to accompany Number 6 on a fishing trip, which in itself plumbed new depths of mind-numbing tedium, it was trying to sleep in a polyester bag within a leaky canvas cocoon that was an altogether more miserable affair. And listening to the sounds of Mother Nature mocking me as I writhed around on the cold, hard floor has left me in little doubt that there is nothing 'great' about the so-called great outdoors, only discomfort and desolation.

DEMOCRACY

A detestable fad.

GAMBLING

I remember the days when gambling was considered urbane. Sitting at the high rollers' blackjack table at the Casino de Monte-Carlo and sipping a Balvenie malt on the rocks in full view of your adoring entourage was the quintessence of sophistication. The same cannot be said of a visit to a high-street bookmaker, where one is routinely surrounded by poor unfortunates riddled with emphysema, who grasp their copies of the *Racing Post* as if it contains the winning lottery numbers. As they skip a hot meal so that they can stake their last few pennies on a 1,000–1 three-legged nag called Rank Outsider, desperation hangs over these pathetic wretches like a pall of sombre fog.

EASTER

I'm not a religious cat, but if I was I'd still find Easter a dubious festivity. For starters, no one really has the faintest idea when it's supposed to take place, which rather makes me question the authenticity of the resurrection of Christ (see *Ghosts*), but it's the

fact that it's become little more than a confectionary binge that has left me most cynical. For example, what exactly is the chocolate egg supposed to signify – that Cadbury had a factory in biblical Nazareth? And what the deuce is the Easter Bunny if not the product of a dangerous imagination?

POLITICAL CORRECTNESS

I'm not sure there's ever been a barrier to ruthless efficiency quite like the crippling cancer that is political correctness. We used to call it as we saw it, and offending someone in the process was a bonus. Nowadays, people consider it necessary to tiptoe around what they really want to say, and for what? What does that ever achieve, apart from awkward confusion and the pointless lengthening of conversation? I've asked our HR department these questions on numerous occasions after being chided for failing to deal with bumbling employees appropriately. Apparently slapping Igor (our web-footed computer analyst) in the face and calling him 'Kermit' was unacceptable, despite the fact that he'd somehow deleted our internal server. Insanity.

VOUCHERS AND COUPONS

You know life has sunk to its nadir when you've ceased to trade in everyday currency and have instead resorted to using vouchers and coupons as your legal tender. Every week these deplorable individuals, typically those found in the saddle of a mobility scooter, arrive at some godforsaken store armed with an array of crudely cut out '25p off own brand' coupons ready to bore the poor till worker responsible for processing them into submission. These are the same folk who scavenge through the sorry-looking shelves of the '£1 shops', or as I call them 'Hell on Earth', feverishly hunting for bargains that will justify their pitiful existences. It sends a chill down my tail just thinking about it.

FASHION

I'm at a loss to explain modern fashion and its none-too-subtle nuances. It strikes me that people no longer take pride in their garb, preferring to bedeck themselves in a manner that suggests they've just absconded from an asylum for the stylishly insane. The evidence is plain enough: surely anyone found wearing a 'onesie' cannot be of sound mind?

ONLINE PETITIONS

A futile exercise if ever there was one. I hoped my legitimate petition would've collected more than the three signatures it ultimately received (and they were all aliases). For the first time ever I wanted to see if taking the moral high ground, without resorting to blackmail and extortion, would fulfil my nefarious schemes. Somewhat unsurprisingly, intimidation seems to be the only language the powers-that-be understand. It's just as well it's my mother tongue.

e-petition created by: **Blofeld's Cat**

Closing: 05/05/2014

Number of signatures: 3

BAN CHINESE LANTERNS!

Providing the main entertainment at a pre-pubescent slumber party would be preferable to observing these preposterous orbs of light floating aimlessly in the night sky. Whilst I'm sure they offer much-needed entertainment in the mundane lives of ordinary folk, these flying death lamps are playing havoc with the aviation tracking equipment at our company headquarters, resulting in us needlessly wasting hundreds of rounds of ammunition in shooting them down and subsequently almost revealing our whereabouts to the local authorities.

If you ever feel the urge to purchase these derisible eyesores, may I suggest indoor fireworks as an alternative? I would far rather you kept your dreary evening's entertainment within the confines of your own home, perhaps even burning it down for good measure.

Blofeld's Cat

CONSPIRACY THEORISTS

I have a natural loathing for these pallid keyboard warriors, who sit behind their laptops in their parents' basements, embalmed in webs of flaky skin, dried seminal fluid and stale food, furiously musing on their online blogs about government assassins and alien invasions. Perhaps my hatred stems from the fact that we've been the victim of these oily individuals in the past, and whilst I enjoyed playing their literal games of 'cat and mouse', it still rankles that we turned these vitamin D-deficient crackpots into martyrs because Number 1 demanded we destroy them. I much preferred the idea of them living in perpetual fear, twitching in terror at the sound of a creaking floorboard or an intimidating text message received at three in the morning.

SKATEBOARDERS

I want to remove their numerous body piercings with a high-powered magnet. Grow up and learn to drive, you grubby oiks! And pull your trousers up – no one wants to see your soiled undergarments.

BARBEQUES

I cannot for the life of me understand the appeal of a barbeque (or BBQ, as they're lovingly referred to by the idiotic enthusiasts who perpetuate them). It's inexplicable to me that people can be excited by the prospect of eating substandard meats, 'cooked' on a substandard appliance, which are more often than not washed down with substandard alcohol. And yet, in one of life's many unfathomable oddities, these substandard affairs are widely celebrated.

No, I don't see these culinary abominations as cause for any celebration whatsoever, unless you have a predilection for scorched pig flesh and salmonella. The sun might be shining, but my spirits certainly won't be.

Actually they will, because I'll be somewhere else.

THE OFFICE CHRISTMAS PARTY

Most of us have been forced to tolerate the dreaded office Christmas party at some point in our lives, the planning of which is made more challenging when one's organisation has been banned from every establishment within a 200-mile radius. But I digress. Watching Barbara from accounts perform her drunken karaoke is tantamount to spending an evening in a vegan restaurant, as is making idle chit-chat with colleagues who are so infernally dull that you literally start sobbing as they regale their plans for the festive season. But nothing is as awkward as fending off the amorous advances of 'Horny' Harriet from admin, who, in an effort to be alluring, once took it upon herself to go skinny-dipping. If only she had remembered it was the piranha pool ∴.

GLOBAL WARMING

I was perfectly content with the notion of global warming as I was under the distinct impression that we would be graced with decades of glorious sunshine and I would be long-dead before the world eventually imploded. However, what I did not sign

up for were cataclysmic floods, icy pellets of death falling from the sky and the general sense of eternal darkness that seem to have sprung straight from the bleakest pages of the Old Testament. Last winter I could've sworn the four horsemen of the apocalypse passed me on the M4 near Windsor. For possibly the first time in my life, I feel myself siding with the hippy protesters. Whatever next?

COWBOY BUILDERS

We recently had an extension built at HQ to allow for the installation of a new canteen (better food, better morale, etc.). However, if I'd have known the stress it would've caused I'd have gladly let our staff continue to suffer malnutrition in their smoky confines.

Such was the brazen manner and impudence of the builders we employed that rather than turning up in a clapped-out Bedford Rascal and wearing baseball caps it would've been more appropriate if they rode in on horseback and sported Stetsons. Indeed, it soon became apparent that they were trying it on at every opportunity, whether it was with their hour-long tea breaks or their relentless wolf-whistling at certain female members of staff, but it was their repeated insistence on calling me 'mate', 'pal' and 'feller' that was the final straw. I am no one's 'mate', as they soon found out when I had them buried alive in the foundations they deemed 'unnecessary'.

COMPUTER GAMES

I would rather suffer an anal prolapse than be coerced into playing a computer game. It beggars belief that some dimwits, who are old enough to know better, can spend hours on end pretending to annihilate their opposition in a tasteless 'shoot 'em up', all the while they become progressively isolated from the real world. They ought to let these pasty-faced recluses experience what it's really like to nervously navigate a sweltering desert full of landmines and merciless militia. I, on the other paw, prefer my life to be entrenched in reality, thus any annihilation on my part usually results in the downfall of a government or the collapse of an economy. It's far more entertaining when it's tangible.

CHARITY

Hell would have to freeze over before I donated to charity. However, I'd be even less inclined to part with my hard-earned money should someone be so foolish as to nominate me to throw myself into a bucket of icy water, withstand a month of sobriety, or take a 'selfie' without my blood diamond-encrusted collar attached. Anyone stupid enough to take part in these asinine japes should be drowned in their own buckets. Now, *that* would be worth donating for ...

CLOWNS

Utter, utter bastards.

CALL CENTRES

They say you should always save your best for last, but in my case I've certainly saved the worst. The one thing guaranteed to get my hackles up above all else is a conversation with a feckless call-centre operative. Is there anything more frustrating and time-consuming? Below is the transcript Number 1 managed to procure following my failed attempt to make a personal injury claim. Should you have a policy with the impossible plebeians that are Broken Bones Insurance, I would strongly recommend you refrain from breaking any bones.

Phone transcript of suspect: SIU3769 34 58

Nitin Bajwa (NB): Good afternoon, thank you for calling Broken Bones Insurance claims department. You're thro-
Blofeld's Cat (BC): (Interrupting) ███████ finally. Four new popes have been elected in the time I've been on hold. And your hold music sounds like a glockenspiel being forcibly inserted into a fox.
NB: OK. You're through to Ronan. Can I take your policy number please?

BC: If your name is Ronan then mine is Angela Lansbury.

NB: Good afternoon, Angela. Can I take your policy number please?

Pause.

BC: XAY1212304B.

NB: Thank you, Angela. For security reasons please can you confirm the first line of your address and postcode?

BC: As you can probably see on your computer and hear from my dulcet tones, my name isn't Angela. It's Blofeld's Cat. I was being sarcastic.

NB: My apologies, Mr Cat. Can I have your address please?

BC: ███ ██████ ████████ ████ Look, I've just been the victim of a hit and run with a blue Ford Fiesta, registration number ███ ██, and I'm fairly certain I've fractured my pelvis. I'm in a lot of pain, so could you please provide me with the details of the reprehensible ██████ who has just tried to destroy me, as I would dearly like to return the favour.

NB: I'm afraid I can't do that, Mr Cat. I strongly advise you speak to the police and go to the hospital to get your injuries examined. We can then process any claim you have.

BC: Come now, Ronan. I'll make it worth your while.

NB: I should warn you that our conversations are recorded, Mr Cat. For training purposes.

BC: Surely your priority should be to cater to the whims of your policy holders, even if they are entirely dishonourable?

NB: Not if it's to help you exact your revenge, Mr Cat. Pause.

BC: I know I'm being recorded, Ronan, so I'll choose my words here carefully. If you don't give me the details of the owner of the blue Ford Fiesta, registration number ███ ███, I will hunt *you* down and disembowel you with a rusty teaspoon. Do you understand what I'm saying?

NB: (Voice wavering) Perhaps you should speak to my manager, Mr Cat?

BC: Perhaps I should.

NB: I'll get him for you now. Thank you for calling Broken Bones Insurance claims department and I hope you have a pleasant day.

BC: ███ you, Ronan.

Long silence in which BC mutters a series of incomprehensible words to himself.

Ravi Purewal (RP) enters the conversation.

RP: Good afternoon, Mr Cat, my name is Steve. How can I help you today?

BC: Right. Firstly, your name isn't Steve. Why you don't just use your real name is beyond me. Secondly, I need you to find me the name and address of the ███ who has just tried to kill me.

And, finally, I want to make a claim.

RP: Please can you provide me with the details of what happened?

BC: Well, my day started off perfectly satisfactorily, but after being mown down in broad daylight by a blue Ford Fiesta, registration number ████ ████, and subsequently having to endure conversations with both you and your intellectually stunted colleague, it's fair to say that things have been going downhill rapidly.

RP: I'm sorry to hear that, Mr Cat, but I won't stand for any abuse of my staff, regardless of your personal circumstances.

BC: I'm just stating the facts, Steve. Your colleague is unreservedly hopeless and you need to fire him. Preferably out of a cannon.

RP: If you require assistance with your injury, you should speak to the police and visit a hospital. We can then deal with your claim once we've seen the medical reports. We can't provide you with any information regarding other parties.

Pause.

BC: Are you happy, Steve?

RP: I beg your pardon?

BC: Are you a happy man? Do you enjoy your job? Do you have a good social life?

RP: Yes, I do.

BC: That's good. Because once I've dealt with the ████████ ████ who just tried to turn me into roadkill, I will come for you, Steve, as well as your slow-witted minion. And I want you both to enjoy your last moments on earth. I have no doubt that I'm calling somewhere in Chandigarh and not Bedford, as advertised on your website, but I'm very well connected and I have a lot of air miles to use up. And I have all the time in the world.

RP: This conversation is being recorded, Mr Cat, and I will be sending it to the relevant authorities for review.

BC: Good. Your successor will know not to fob me off the next time I call. And I will call, Steve.

RP: Goodbye, Mr Cat.

BC: Goodbye, Steve. Sleep with one eye open.

End of conversation

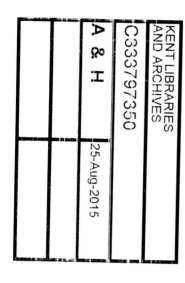